D1278616

Strictly Classics

Ensemble Arrangements of 14 Classic Favorites that correlate with Book 2 of *Strictly Strings*

JOHN O'REILLY

Each of the ensembles in this collection is correlated to specific pages in Book 2 of the *Strictly Strings* method. These arrangements will not only motivate beginning string students in the classroom, but will also encourage home chamber music sessions.

Each of the four instruments is divided into two parts—part A and part B. Each instrument's part A contains the melody. For the Violin and Viola, part B is a harmony line, and for the Cello and Bass, it is the bass part. This flexible format also includes a simple piano accompaniment.

Contents

Instrumentation

Violin   Viola   Cello   Bass
Piano Accompaniment   Conductor's Score

Cover photo: String Section of the London Symphony Orchestra • Clive Barda / Performing Arts Library
Cover design: Candace Smith

HIGHLAND/ETLING
A DIVISION OF Alfred

Finale from the *Surprise Symphony*

Franz Joseph Haydn

Andante

Wolfgang Amadeus Mozart

Andante

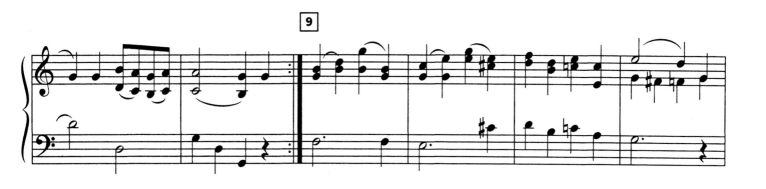

Emperor Waltz

Johann Strauss

Two Schumann Favorites
Traumerai

Robert Schumann

Soldier's March

Allegro moderato

Bourrée

George F. Handel

March in D Major

Johann Sebastian Bach

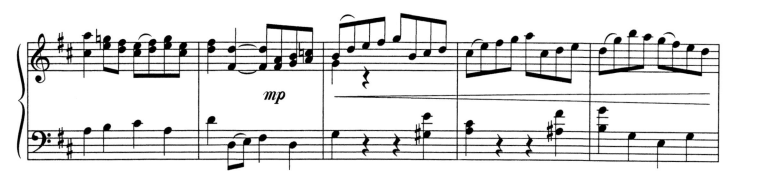

Hunter's Chorus

from *Der Freischutz*

Carl Maria von Weber

Trumpet Tune

Henry Purcell

Two Handel Favorites
The Harmonious Blacksmith

George F. Handel

Bourrée
from *Water Music*

Minuet in G

Ludwig van Beethoven

Moderato

D. C. al Fine

Nocturne and March

from *A Midsummer Night's Dream*

Nocturne

Felix Mendelssohn

10

March

Procession of the Sardar

Ippolitov Ivanov

Rondo

Henry Purcell

Three Mozart Minuets
I.

Wolfgang Amadeus Mozart

II.

Moderato

III.

Moderato